God Danced the Day You Were Born

humor and wisdom for celebrating life

PuddleDancer PRESS™

Created by Meiji Stewart

Illustrated by David Blaisdell

God Danced the Day You Were Born
© 1997 by Meiji Stewart

ISBN# 0-9647349-7-4

PuddleDancer Press is an imprint of the
Keep Coming Back Company.
Published in Del Mar, California
P. O. Box 1204, Del Mar, California 92014
1-800-522-3383

1st Printing

Illustration: David Blaisdell, Tucson, Arizona
Cover illustraion and design: Kahn Design, Encinitas, California
Book design: Roger Krueger, San Diego, California
Printing: Dickinson Press, Grand Rapids, Michigan

Dedicated to my family, who mean the world to me:
My mother, Nanette, and father, Richard, my grandmother
Mary, my sister, Leslie, my brothers, Ray and Scott, my
nephews and nieces Sebastien, Emilie, Skye, Luke, Jake,
Nanette, Cairo and Kamana, and to Fumi, Jocelyne, Richard
and Stephen. And especially to my daughter Malia (the
puddledancer), and her loving mom, Julie.

Thanks to:
David for the wonderful illustrations. I am truly blessed to be
able to work with him. Thanks also to Roger for putting it all
together, almost always under deadline (usually yesterday).
Thanks to Jeff for the delightful book covers, and, even more,
for his friendship. Thanks to Zane, Regina, Jan, Gay and Jane
for all you do and for being so loving and caring. And a very
special thanks to my mom and dad for encouraging me to
believe in and pursue my dreams.

Don't look for miracles.
You are a miracle.

Every human being is a spark
that wants to burst into flame.

Reshad Feild

4

Celebrate yourself. God made you
exactly as he wanted you to be.

You have a unique message to deliver,
a unique song to sing,
a unique act of love to bestow.
This message, this song,
and this act of love have been entrusted
exclusively to the one and only you.

John Powell

Don't hide your light under a lampshade.

Do not compare yourself with others, for you are a unique and wonderful creation. Make your own beautiful footprints in the snow. *Barbara Kimball*

Smile, God loves you.

A friend is able to see you as the
wonderful person God created you to be.

Ann D. Parrish

We are each of us angels with only one wing, and we can only fly embracing each other. *Luciano De Crescenzo*

If you begin to live life looking
for all the good that is around you,
you will find joy everywhere.

When you affirm big,
believe big,
and pray big,
big things happen.

Norman Vincent Peale

God is the silent partner in all great enterprises.
Abraham Lincoln

Everyone has inside of him a piece of good news.
The good news is that you don't know how great
you can be! How much you can love!
What you can accomplish!
And what your potential is!

Anne Frank

Be the cause of wonderful things.

Practice Random Kindness and Senseless Acts of Beauty.
Ann Herbert

No matter what age you are,
or what your circumstances might be,
you are special and still have something unique to
offer. Your life, because of who you are, has meaning.

Barbara De Angelis

Memories, important yesterdays, were once todays.
Treasure and notice today.

Gloria Gaither

We all have possibilities we don't know about.
We can do things we don't even dream we can do.
Dale Carnegie

Today is the tomorrow you worried about yesterday,
and all is well.

God says to me with kind of a smile,
"Hey, how would you like to be
in charge for awhile and steer the world?"
"Okay" says I, "I'll give it a try. Where do I sit?
How much do I get? What time is lunch? When can I quit?"
"I'll take back the wheel", says God,
"I don't think you're quite ready yet."

Don't try to force anything.
Let life be a deep let-go.
See God opening millions of flowers
every day without forcing the buds.

Bhagwan Shree Rajneesh

When I tune into my beautiful self, I get happiness.
Everything in the universe belongs to me.

Dick Gregory

Something wonderful, something hidden.
A gift unique to you. Find it.

Ralph Waldo Emerson

You are one of a kind;
therefore, no one can really predict
to what heights you might soar.
Even you will not know
until you spread your wings!

Gil Atkinson

God's door is always open.

Hold fast your dreams!
Within your heart keep one still, secret spot
where dreams may go and sheltered so,
may thrive and grow.

Louise Driscoll

Remember that you are unique.
If that is not fulfilled,
then something wonderful has been lost.

Martha Graham

Dreams come a size too big so that
we can grow into them. *Josie Bisset*

God puts each fresh morning,
each new chance of life,
into our hands as a gift
to see what we will do with it.

Today a new sun rises for me,
everything lives, everything is animated,
everything seems to speak to me of my passion,
everything invites me to cherish it....

Anne de Lenclos

22

I would rather live in a world where my life is surrounded by mystery than live in a world so small that my mind could comprehend it. *Henry Emerson Fosdick*

This moment—this day—is as good as any moment in all eternity. I shall make of this day—each moment of this day—a heaven on earth.

Dan Custer

If you were arrested for being kind to others, would there be enough evidence to convict you?

Loving someone is seeing them the way God intended.

Everything God does is love—
even when we do not understand him.

Basilea Schlink

Dear God, I pray for patience,
And I want it right now!

Oren Arnold

God's "no" is simply a prelude to a much bigger "yes."

I change myself,
I change the world.

Gloria Anzaldua

A human is a single being.
Unique and unrepeatable.

John Paul II

I am not a has-been. I'm a will be.
Helen Hayes

Give to every other human being
every right you claim for yourself.

Robert G. Ingersoll

"Your task, to build a better world," God said.
I answered, "How? This world is such a large,
vast place, so complicated now, and I so small
and useless am, there's nothing I can do."
But God in all his wisdom said, "Just build a better you...
You must do the thing you think you cannot do."

Eleanor Roosevelt

There is no limit to God's love.
It is without measure and
its depth cannot be sounded.

Mother Teresa

I wish you all the joy you can wish.

William Shakespeare

My religion is very simple—my religion is kindness.

The Dalai Lama

On the street I saw a small girl cold and shivering in
a thin dress, with little hope of a decent meal.
I became angry and said to God:
"Why did you permit this?
Why don't you do something about it?"
For a while God said nothing.
That night God replied quite suddenly:
"I certainly did something about it. I made you."

If you want my final opinion on the mystery of life and all that, I can give it to you in a nutshell. The universe is like a safe to which there is a combination. But the combination is locked up in the safe. *Peter De Vries*

God loves each one of us,
as if there were only one of us.

St. Augustine

May the sun always shine on your windowpane;
May a rainbow be certain to follow each rain.
May the hand of a friend always be near you;
May God fill your heart with gladness to cheer you.

Irish Blessing

Falling in love with God is the greatest romance.

Look for the heaven here on earth.
It is all around you.

People see God everyday.
They just don't recognize him.

Pearl Bailey.

One cannot collect all the beautiful shells on the beach, one can collect only a few. *Anne Morrow Lindbergh*

Think of yourself as on the
threshold of unparalleled success.
A whole clear, glorious life lies before you.

Andrew Carnegie

There is nothing which God cannot accomplish.

Cicero

God will help you if you try, and you can
if you think you can. *Anna Delaney Peale*

A tulip doesn't strive to impress anyone.
It doesn't struggle to be different than a rose.
It doesn't have to. It is different.
And there's room in the garden for every flower.

Marianne Williamson

I consider myself a Christian, Hindu,
Moslem, Jew, Buddhist, and Confucian.

Mohandes Gandhi

We are all God's children.

Life is what we are alive to.
It is not length but breadth...
Be alive to... goodness, kindness,
purity, love, history, poetry, music,
flowers, stars, God, and eternal hope.

Maltbie Babcock

We are such stuff as dreams are made of.

William Shakespeare

42

Nobody succeeds beyond his or her wildest
expectations unless he or she begins with
some wild expectations. *Ralph Charell*

Happiness depends not upon
things around me, but on my attitude.
Everything in my life will depend on my attitude.

Alfred A. Montapert

If spring came but once in a century instead of
once a year, or burst forth with the sound of
an earthquake and not in silence, what
wonder and expectation there would be in all
hearts, to behold the miraculous change.

Henry Wadsworth Longfellow

Something deep in all of us yearns for God's beauty,
and we can find it no matter where we are.

Sue Monk Kidd

Stand outside this evening.
Look at the stars.
Know that you are special and
loved by the One who created them.

God's alarm clock has no snooze button.

God has put into each of our lives a void
that cannot be filled by the world.
We may leave God or put him on hold,
but he is always there, patiently waiting for us...
to turn back to him.

Emilie Barnes

46

Lord, I shall be very busy this day. I may forget thee, but do not thou forget me. *Sir Jacob Astley*

A friend is a present you give yourself.

Robert Louis Stevenson

When God conceived the world, that was poetry;
He formed it, and that was sculpture;
He varied and colored it, and that was painting;
and then, crowning all, He peopled it with living
beings, and that was the grand divine, eternal drama.

Charlotte Cushman

I didn't find my friends; the good God gave them to me.

Ralph Waldo Emerson

Snuggle in God's arms.
When you are hurting, when you feel lonely...
let Him cradle you, comfort you,
reassure you of His all-sufficient power and love.

Kay Arthur

Even when all we see are the tangled threads
on the backside of life's tapestry,
we know that God is good
and is out to do us good always.

Richard Foster

Let go and let God be in charge.

The intense desire for God realization
is itself the way to it.

Sri Anandamayi Ma

The journey is the reward.

Tao saying

Seeking God is the greatest adventure.

I wondered why somebody didn't do something;
then I realized that I was somebody.

God shall be my hope, my stay,
my guide and lantern to my feet.

William Shakespeare

Remember the faith that moves
mountains always carries a pick.

Celebrate! Celebrate! Life is a celebration!

The future is as bright as the promises of God.
We know not what the future holds,
but we know who holds the future.

Robert C. Savage

We are God's melody of life;
She sings Her song through us.

Somewhere on the great world the sun is always shining, and just as sure as you live, it will sometime shine on you. The dear God made it so. There is so much sunshine we must all have our share.

Myrtle Reed

Prayer is the peace of our spirit,
the stillness of our thoughts,
the evenness of our recollection,
the sea of our meditation,
the rest of our cares,
and the calm of our tempest.

Jeremy Taylor

Abandon yourself utterly for the love of God,
and in this way
you will become truly happy.

Henry Suso

O Lord, help me to be pure, but not yet.

St. Augustine

Please do not feel personally, totally, irrevocably responsible for everything. That's my job, Love, God.

We have a God who delights in impossibilities.

Give your troubles to God.
God will be up all night anyway.

The grace of God means something like:
Here is your life. You might never have been,
but you are because the party wouldn't have been
complete without you. Here is the world.
Beautiful and terrible things will happen.
Don't be afraid. I am with you. Nothing can ever
separate us. It's for you I created the universe.
I love you...

Frederick Buechner

God always leaves the porch light on.

I love these little people;
and it is not a slight thing,
when they, who are so fresh from God,
love us.

Charles Dickens.

Of all nature's gifts to the human race,
what is sweeter to a man than his children?

Cicero

Parenthood is a partnership with God... you are working with the Creator of the universe in shaping human character and determining destiny. *Ruth Vaughn*

I love to think of nature as an unlimited
broadcasting station through which God speaks
to us every hour, if only we will tune in.

George Washington Carver

Fling the door of your heart
wide open and let God in.
If you learn to do that,
everything you touch all day long
will be stamped with the presence of God.

God loves me... God loves me... God loves me...

With God, the difficult we do right away,
the impossible may take a little longer.

Courage and perseverance have a magical talisman,
before which difficulties disappear and obstacles
vanish into air.

John Quincy Adams

68

Sometimes you just have to take the leap
and build your wings on the way down. *Kobi Yamada*

We are the hero of our own story.

Mary McCarthy

Our God is so wonderfully good and
lovely and blessed in every way that the
mere fact of belonging to him is enough
for an untellable fullness of joy!

Hannah Whiteall Smith

Every child comes with the message that God is not yet discouraged of Mankind. *Rabindranath Tagore*

I Am...

Amazing, the architect of my destiny. • Beautiful, both inside and out. • Courageous, being true to myself. • Dynamic, constantly changing and growing. • Enlightened, knowing all is well in the world. • Fallible, perfectly imperfect. • Grateful, for each and every day. • Healthy, full of energy. Intuitive, honoring the still small voice within. Joyful, celebrating the truth of my being. Kindhearted, reaching out to others. • Lovable, exactly as I am. • Miraculous, a precious child of the universe. • **N**ow Here, fully in this moment. **O**ptimistic, anything is possible. • **P**rosperous, manifesting abundance. • **Q**uick to build bridges, not walls. • **R**esourceful, obstacles are my stepping stones. • **S**piritual, having a human experience. • **T**rustworthy, speaking the language of the heart. • **U**nique, the only me there is, was, or ever will be. • **V**aluable, I make a difference. **W**ise, open to all of life's lessons. • **X**cited, about living and loving life. • **Y**oung At Heart, delightfully childlike. • **Z**estful, happy to be me!

73

My friend shall forever be my friend,
and reflect a ray of God to me.

Henry David Thoreau

The entire sum of existence
is the magic of being needed by just one person.

Vi Putnam

I'm so glad you are here.... It helps me to realize how beautiful my world is. *Rainer Maria Rilke*

God's bright sunshine overhead,
God's flowers beneath your feet,
the path of life that you must tread...
And by such pleasant pathways led,
may all your life be sweet.

Helen Wraithman

True happiness depends upon
close alliance with God.

There is no right way to pray. Only your way.

We are not human beings having a spiritual experience.
We are spiritual beings having a human experience.

Ram Dass

Remember your label:
"Made by God."

Angels can fly because they take themselves lightly. *G.K. Chesterton*

There are four ways God answers prayer:
No, not yet;
No, I love you too much;
Yes, I thought you'd never ask;
Yes, and here's more.

Ann Lewis

When we call on God,
he bends down his ear to listen,
as a father bends down to listen to his little child.

Elizabeth Charles

Our need is God's opportunity.

Expect great things from God.
Attempt great things for God.

William Carey

The purpose of life is to matter,
to count, to stand for something,
to have it make some difference
that we have lived at all.

Leo Buscaglia

We can paint a great picture on a small canvas.

C.D. Warner

The sun does not rise
because of the rotation of the earth.
The sun rises because God says to it," Get up."

G.K.Chesterton

Just to be is a blessing.
Just to live is holy.

Rabbi Abraham Heschel

Where others see but the dawn coming over the hill, I see the soul of God shouting for joy. *William Blake*

Happiness is neither within us only, or without us;
it is the union of ourselves with God.

Blaise Pascal

For all that has been, Thanks.
For all that will be,Yes.

Dag Hammarskjold

O God, I have tasted thy goodness,
and it has both satisfied me
and made me thirsty for more.

A. W. Tozer

I thank You God for this most amazing day;
for the leaping spirits of trees
and a blue true dream of sky;
and for everything which is natural
which is infinite which is yes.

e.e. cummings

May the road rise to meet you,
may the wind be always at your back,
may the sun shine warm upon your face,
may the rain fall soft upon your fields
and until we meet again
may God hold you in the palm of His hand.

An Irish Blessing

We all have possibilities we don't know about.
We can do things we don't even dream we can do.

Dale Carnegie

I find the great thing in this world is not so much
where we stand, as in what direction we are moving:
To reach the port of Heaven we must sail, sometimes
with the wind and sometime against it—but we must
sail, not drift or lie at anchor. *Oliver Wendell Holmes, Jr.*

God knows no distance.

Charleszetta Waddles

God is the sunshine that warms us,
the rain that melts the frost
and waters young plants.
The presence of God is a climate of
strong and bracing love, always there.

Joan Arnold

There's always room at the top.
Daniel Webster

Deep within you is everything that is perfect,
ready to radiate through you and out into the world.

We are what and where we are
because we have first imagined it.

Donald Curtis

Life is something like this trumpet.
If you don't put anything in it you don't get
anything out. And that's the truth. *W. C. Handy*

What lies behind us,
and what lies before us are tiny matters,
compared to what lies within us.

Ralph Waldo Emerson

God created us with an overwhelming desire to soar...
He designed us to be tremendously productive
and "to mount up with wings like eagles,"
realistically dreaming of what
he can do with our potential.

Carol Kent

With God anything is possible.

I know God will not give me anything I can't handle.
I just wish that He didn't trust me so much.

Mother Teresa

God, I know you're not in a hurry.
Your plans for me are on time.
You need no schedule or reminders
for I'm always on your mind.

Elain Wright Colvin

If God is your co-pilot—move over.

If God expresses through you,
is God having a good time?

Christian Sorenson

The sun shines not on us, but in us.

John Muir

If you live close to God and His infinite grace,
You don't have to tell, it shows on your face.

God made me—I was no accident, no happenstance. I was in God's plan, and God doesn't make junk. I was born to be a successful human being; I am somebody special, unique, definitely one of a kind, and I love me. That is essential, so that I might love others also. I have talents and potential. Yes, there is greatness in me, and if I harness my special qualities, then I will write my name in the sands of time with my deeds. Yes, I must work hard and long, and with great drive if I am to excel. I will pay that price. Talents demand daily care and honing. I was born in God's image and likeness. I will strive to do God's will.

Life is God's gift to you.
The way you live your life is your gift to God.
Make it a fantastic one.

Leo Buscaglia

There are many wonderful things
that will never be done if you do not do them.

Honorable Charles D. Gill

101

God gave us memory
that we might have roses in December.

James M. Barrie

As a rose fills a room with its fragrance,
so will God's love fill our lives.

Margaret Brownley

I am a little pencil in the hand of a writing God who is sending a love letter to the world. *Mother Teresa*

Because I love God, I can love you.
Because God cares for me, I can care for you.

Gayle Roper

Joy is the echo of God's life within us.

Joseph Marmion

Friendship is God's special way of
loving us through someone else.

If only God would give me some clear sign!
Like making a large deposit in my name
at a Swiss bank.

Woody Allen

In my soul I know that God knows me and loves me,
and loves me even though he knows me.
My heart has every reason to smile.

Greg Anderson

If you judge people, you have no time to love them.
Mother Teresa

All the things in this world are
gifts and signs of God's love to us.
The whole world is a love letter from God.

Peter Kreeft

Never lose an opportunity of
seeing anything that is beautiful;
for beauty is God's handwriting—
a wayside sacrament.

Ralph Waldo Emerson

As the old man walked the beach at dawn, he noticed a young man ahead of him picking up starfish and flinging them into the sea. Finally catching up with the youth, he asked him why he was doing this. The answer was that the stranded starfish would die if left until the morning sun "But the beach goes on for miles and there are millions of starfish," countered the other. "How can your effort make any difference?" The young man looked at the starfish in his hand and then threw it to safety in the waves. "It makes a difference to that one, " he said. *Minnesota Literacy Council*

To see God in everything makes life
the greatest adventure there is.

Jo Petty

Be assured that if God waits longer than you wish,
it is only to make the blessing all the more precious.

Andrew Murray

When God closes a door, He usually opens a window.
Robert Owens

God loves us so much that sometimes
He gives us what we need and not what we ask.

Max Lucado

Lord, I am so grateful that though
I am not able to choose my circumstances,
I can choose the attitude with which I react to them,
and so I choose to be happy... .
because You have not forgotten me.

Ralph Waldo Emerson

If you can't be thankful for what you receive,
be thankful for what you escape.

Give to the world the best you have,
and the best will come back to you.

Janet L. Weaver

Every morning is a fresh opportunity to find God's
extraordinary joy in the most ordinary places.

Janet L. Weaver

Let us open up our natures,
throw wide the doors of our hearts and
let in the sunshine of good will and kindness.

O. S. Marden

God is so big
He can cover the whole world with His love,
and so small He can curl up inside your heart.

The fullness of joy is to behold God in everything.

Julian of Norwich

Each second we live is a
unique moment of the universe—
a moment that never was before
and will never be again.

Pablo Casals

Joy is what happens to us when we allow ourselves to recognize how good things really are. *Marianne Williamson*

May God's richest blessing
be upon you today and throughout the year—
and may those blessings flow through you
to touch the lives of everyone you meet.

Gary Smalley

Faith isn't the ability to believe
long and far into the misty future.
It's simply taking God at His word
and taking the next step.

Joni Eareckson Tada

If you go to God with a thimble, you can only bring back a thimbleful. *Randolph Wilkerson.*

Heaven is here.
There is no other place.
Heaven is now.
There is no other time.

A Course in Miracles

Imagine the joy of day by day growing
into a fuller understanding of who you are—
who you are, really, the power you really have.

Tae Yun Kim

If I had a single flower for every time I think about you,
I could walk forever in my garden. *Claudia Grandi*

Be not simply good;
be good for something.

Thoreau

Every single act of love
bears the imprint of God.

Goodness is the only investment that never fails.

H.D. Thoreau

Life is not always what one wants it to be,
but to make the best of it as it is,
is the only way of being happy.

Jennie Jerome Churchill

Reach up as far as you can,
and God will reach down all the way.

John H. Vincent

We learn as much from sorrow as from joy, as much from illness as from health, from handicap as from advantage—and indeed perhaps more. *Pearl Buck*

Do not try to imitate the lark
or the nightingale, if you can't do it.
If it's your destiny to croak like a toad,
then go ahead! And with all your might!
Make them hear you!

Louis-Ferdinand Celine

Everyone has their own specific vocation or mission
in life... Therein, we cannot be replaced, nor can our
lives be repeated. Thus, everyone's task is as unique
as their specific opportunity to implement it.

Victor Frankl

God gives us the ingredients for our daily bread,
but expects us to do the baking.

The more I study nature
the more I am amazed at the Creator.

Louis Pasteur

Your daily life is your temple and your religion.
When you enter into it, take with you your all.

Kahlil Gibran

At every moment the universe
is making you an irresistible offer.

Prayer is exhaling the spirit of man
and inhaling the spirit of God.

Edwin Keith

Know that you yourself are a miracle.

Dr. Norman Vincent Peale

Start a crusade in your life—to dare to be your best.

William Danforth

Better to keep yourself clean and bright, you are the
window through which you must see the world.

I am larger, better than I thought.
I did not know I held so much goodness.

Walt Whitman

Each of us is great insofar as we perceive
and act on the infinite possibilities which lie
undiscovered and unrecognized about us.

James Harvey Robinson

When two people relate to each other authentically and humanly, God is the electricity that surges between them. *Martin Buber*

God sends the brilliant light of a rainbow
to remind us of His presence.

Verdell Davis

That I am here is a wonderful mystery
to which I will respond with joy.

Who so draws nigh to God one step through doubtings dim, God will advance a mile in blazing light to him.

If you have succeeded in getting
hold of Almighty God's hand, don't let it go.
Keep hold of him by constantly renewing...
prayers to him, acts of desire,
and the seeking to please him in little things.

Mother Francis Raphael

You pay God a compliment by asking great things of him.

Teresa of Avila

The winds of grace blow all the time. All
we need to do is set our sails. *Ramakrishna*

The real voyage of discovery consists
not in seeking new landscapes,
but in having new eyes.

Marcel Proust

May you always find
new roads to travel,
new horizons to explore,
new dreams to call your own.

Two roads diverged in a wood, and I—I took the one less traveled by, and that has made all the difference. *Robert Frost*

What you are doing I may not be able to do...
What I am doing you may not be able to do...
but all of us together are doing something
beautiful for God.

Mother Teresa

Of all the earthly music
that which reaches furthest into Heaven
is the beating of a truly loving heart.

Henry Ward Beecher

Friends are gifts from God. Treasure them.

Everyone needs reminders that
the fact of their being on this earth is important,
and that each life changes everything.

Marge Kennedy

May God give you eyes to see beauty
only the heart can understand.

Live your life while you have it.
Life is a splendid gift—
there is nothing small about it.

Florence Nightingale

It only takes a spark to get a fire going,
And soon all those around can warm up in its glowing;
that's how it is with God's love,
once you've experienced it;
you spread His love to everyone,
you want to pass it on.

Kurt Kaiser

Give thanks for unknown blessings
already on their way.

Native American Saying

You are a reservoir with a
limited amount of resources;
you are a channel attached
to unlimited divine resources.

God warms His hands at man's heart when he prays. *John Masefield.*

Say you are well, and all is well with you,
and God will hear your words and make them true.

James Russell Lowell

To you I'm an atheist.
To God I'm the loyal opposition.

Woody Allen

Bask in God's love.

How beautiful it is to be alive!

Henry Septimus Sutton

May you grow to be as beautiful
as God meant you to be when
He first thought of you.

148

God made you an original, not a copy. Be yourself.

God is and all is well

John Greenleaf Whittier

Be thou the rainbow to the storms of life!

George Gordon Byron

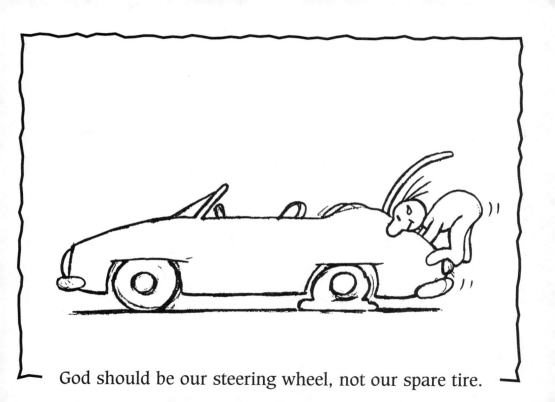

God should be our steering wheel, not our spare tire.

All we have and are is a gift of grace to be shared.

Lloyd John Ogilvie

God's in his heaven—all's right with the world!

Robert Browning

Each one of us is God's special work of art,
a painting like no other in all of time. *Joni Eareckson Tada*

When Life Gives you Lemons...
and other recipes for living & loving life

Thought-provoking, attitude-changing wonderful recipes on how to make the best from the "wurst" of any situation. Accepting challenges and overcoming adversity can lead to greater self-esteem, self-acceptance and self-discovery.

A uniquely illustrated "you can if you think you can" book to empower anybody – student, co-worker, relative, friend, partner, child – to aspire to, believe in, and pursue their dreams. Go for it! Life is not a dress rehearsal.

Shoot For The Moon
Even if you miss you'll land among the stars.

It's a Jungle Out There!

The best survival kit for living and loving in the jungle of every day life. Great line drawings and timeless truths to offer hope and encouragement for anyone facing the daily challenges of our fast-paced stress-filled society.

Happiness is a choice. Pass it on! Really knowing we all have the power to choose happiness at any moment, in any situation, is truly empowering. This book is a great reminder that happiness is found right here, right now.

Happiness is an Inside Job

Humor & wisdom celebrating the art of happiness

A wondrous gift for anybody interested in the well-being of children. This delightfully illustrated book uses wisdom from the ages and poignant humor to encourage everyone, especially parents and teachers, to love, cherish, and honor children.

Parenting, the ultimate adventure. Raising a child can be life's most demanding and extraordinary challenge and also its greatest happiness. A perfect gift for parents, grandparents, teachers and child care providers

Let go and let God.
Please do not feel personally,
totally, irrevocably responsible
for everything. That's my job.
Love, God.
Help someone receive
understanding, insight and
support to face life's challenges.

Dare to follow your heart's
desire... Dare to harvest your
dreams... Dare to speak your
truth... Dare to nurture your
spirit... An ideal gift book to
encourage anybody to aspire to,
believe in and pursue dreams.

"I Am..." on pages 72–73
is part of our A-Z series of gift products.
Other A-Z titles include:

- Children Are
- Children Need
- Dare To
- Fathers Are
- Friends Are
- Happiness Is
- Mothers Are
- Recovery Is

These unique sayings and many other empowering designs are available on a variety of items, including bookmarks, wallet cards and greeting cards.Please call for a complimentary catalog.

PuddleDancer PRESS™

P.O. Box 1204, Del Mar, California 92014
1-800-522-3383

Qty.	Title	Item #	Unit Cost	Total
	Relax, God is in Charge	BK01	6.95	
	Keep Coming Back	BK02	6.95	
	Children are Meant to be Seen & Heard	BK03	6.95	
	Shoot for the Moon	BK04	6.95	
	When Life Gives You Lemons...	BK05	6.95	
	It's a Jungle Out There	BK06	6.95	
	Parenting... Part Joy... Part Guerrilla Warfare	BK07	6.95	
	God Danced the Day You WereBorn	BK08	6.95	
	Happiness is an Inside Job	BK09	6.95	
	Anything is Possible	BK10	6.95	

Tax Help:
Tax on a 6.95 book is 0.54

Subtotal
Shipping & Handling (info below)
CA residents (only) add 7.75% tax
Total

PuddleDancer PRESS

Send books to:

Name _____

Address _____

City_____ State____ Zip _____

Phone (_____)_____

Payment via:

☐ Check/money order

☐ VISA   ☐ Mastercard   ☐ AMEX

Acct#_____Exp. Date _____

Signature_____

Yes! Please send me the books indicated above. Add $2.00 shipping and handling for the first book and 50¢ for each additional book. Add $2.50 extra to the total for books shipped to Canada. Overseas orders to be paid by credit card. Allow up to four weeks for delivery. Send check or money order payable to **Keep Coming Back**. No cash or C.O.D.'s, please. Prices subject to change without notice. Quantity discount available upon request.

Mail to: Keep Coming Back, P.O. Box 1204, Del Mar, California 92014
Call: Local: 619.452.1386   Fax: 619.452.2797   Toll-free **800.522.3383**

PuddleDancer PRESS™

Complimentary Catalog Available
P.O. Box 1204, Del Mar, California 92014   1-800-522-3383

PuddleDancer titles available from your favorite bookstore:

Relax, God is in Charge	ISBN 0-9647349-0-7
Keep Coming Back	ISBN 0-9647349-1-5
Children are Meant to be Seen and Heard	ISBN 0-9647349-2-3
Shoot for the Moon	ISBN 0-9647349-3-1
When Life Gives You Lemons…	ISBN 0-9647349-4-X
It's a Jungle Out There!	ISBN 0-9647349-5-8
Parenting… Part Joy… Part Guerrilla Warfare	ISBN 0-9647349-6-6
God Danced the Day You Were Born	ISBN 0-9647349-7-4
Happiness is an Inside Job	ISBN 0-9647349-8-2
Anything is Possible	ISBN 0-9647349-9-0

Acknowledgements
Every effort has been made to find the copyright owner of the material used. However, there are a few quotations that have been impossible to trace, and we would be glad to hear from the copyright owners of these quotations, so that acknowledgement can be recognized in any future edition.